Autumn
Testament

James K. Baxter

Autumn Testament

Edited by PAUL MILLAR

Auckland

OXFORD UNIVERSITY PRESS

Oxford Melbourne New York

OXFORD UNIVERSITY PRESS NEW ZEALAND

Oxford New York
Athens Auckland Bangkok Bogota Bombay Buenos Aires
Calcutta Cape Town Dar es Salaam Delhi
Florence Hong Kong Istanbul Karachi
Kuala Lumpur Madras Madrid Melbourne
Mexico City Nairobi Paris Port Moresby
Singapore Taipei Tokyo Toronto Warsaw
and associated companies in
Berlin Ibadan

OXFORD is a trade mark of Oxford University Press

ISBN 019 558386 8

Edited by Cathryn Game
Cover design by Anitra Blackford
Front cover photograph: *New Zealand Herald*
Back cover photograph: Ans Westra
Typeset by Anitra Blackford
Printed by CTPS, Hong Kong
Published by Oxford University Press
540 Great South Road, Greenlane, PO Box 11-149,
Auckland, New Zealand

Contents

Preface

This edition aims to reproduce as faithfully as possible the text of the Price Milburn edition of *Autumn Testament*. The only substantial changes from that edition involve the replacement of Frank McKay's tribute by an introductory essay and minor corrections to the word order in the glossary.

My thanks to Jacquie Baxter, Kathleen Coleridge, Geoffrey Miles, Bruce Morrison, Vincent O'Sullivan, Hugh Price, the Hocken Library, and the Victoria University of Wellington Library. I am particularly grateful to my father, Graham Millar, for his knowledge and interest, and my wife, Kay, for her valuable comments.

Introduction

On the evening of 22 October 1972, James K. Baxter began experiencing the early stages of a heart attack. He was in Auckland at the time, waiting at medical rooms for his doctor, who had left him briefly to visit another patient. Deciding to call his friend Jean Tuwhare for help, Baxter crossed to a house on the other side of the street to ask if he could use the telephone. After making the call, his condition worsened, and the owners of the house, Vonney and Bruce Allan, invited him to lie down on their living-room sofa. A while later he died. He was forty-six years old.

At his death, Baxter was in the company of his doctor, Jean Tuwhare, and the sympathetic Allans.[1] Yet second-hand accounts of the event make it seem that his remark in *Jerusalem Daybook*, 'I may die without company', had been prophetic.[2] Stories of him dying alone—even rejected by those from whom he sought help—gained some currency, perhaps because they fitted so well with one of his favourite personae, that of the lone poet rejected by a society unable to stomach its disturbing reflection in his work. The man who had written, 'I can't demythologise [my life]. What happens is either meaningless to me, or else it is mythology'[3] might even have enjoyed the fact that others would find it difficult to demythologise his death.

There is a close connection between Baxter's death and the publication of *Autumn Testament*. When he died a shock wave rippled through New Zealand, and there was the appearance of genuine mourning and grief across the nation. The *Dominion* billboard of 24 October summed up the mood succinctly:

James K. Baxter
Friend
1926–1972

Grief was not merely the preserve of Baxter's closest associates—his family, Catholic priests, artists, writers, alcoholics, hippies, academics, and so on. Many 'ordinary' New Zealanders seemed to feel that their society was poorer without him. Numerous people, in a uniquely Kiwi version of the 'Kennedy effect', remember where they were and what they were doing when they heard he had died.

Days later *Autumn Testament* was rolling off the presses of Price Milburn's printer. Given the proximity of the two events, it is not surprising that Baxter's last book should have been seized on as carrying an elevated significance.[4] Frank McKay's prefatory tribute, written a week after Baxter's tangi, helped to establish a tone of piety towards the volume that most of its reviewers were prepared to follow. His disclosure that 'at the time of his death [Baxter] was correcting the proofs' gave *Autumn Testament* the credibility of a dying man's last words. McKay's expression of the 'agony of [Baxter's] dying' that already 'gives way to peace' was taken as licence to personalise one's response to this 'noble testament' from a poet whose 'life became the poetry'. Thus the tone of the *Sunday Times* reviewer is of an intimate friend, commenting on the hypocrisy of fellow mourners, when he notes that in death Baxter 'seems to have been universally canonised, as if eulogies could in some way make up for past disdain'. The review goes on to rate *Autumn Testament* 'one of [Baxter's] finest works', where beliefs appear in 'blinding clarity … as if before his death all his ideas and teachings had certainly converged into a central, clear theme'.[5] The reviewer for the *Dominion*, perhaps sparked by McKay's comments regarding Baxter's expression of 'his achieved religious faith', conscripted a religious simile to describe the components of this 'last epistle from Jerusalem' as being like 'beads of a rosary, incantations of a litany'.[6]

It is easy, twenty-five years later, when attempting to disentangle the events of Baxter's death and the publication of his final work, to find McKay's introduction overstated. C.K. Stead's criticism of the 'brief tribute' as 'unfortunate and something of an obstacle at the front' of *Autumn Testament* has some point.[7] The value of McKay's words now is as part of the historical record. In their immediacy and intimacy they convey the extent of the loss felt by Baxter's closest friends.

Some reviewers of *Autumn Testament* balanced emotion and judgement. Howard McNaughton, for example, commenced his piece for the *Christchurch Press* with the cautionary comment that as this 'is the last volume which James K. Baxter prepared before his death … most readers will probably find it impossible to approach it with much objectivity'.[8]

No one, however, approached the work with anything like the objectivity of Baxter himself when he forwarded the manuscript to his publisher. In early March 1972 an envelope addressed to Hugh Price was received at the Wellington office of publishers Price Milburn. Inside was a manuscript and a brief covering letter in Baxter's legible, if somewhat untidy, handwriting:

Dear Hughie—

Book of sorts. Only copy—have lost the ms. Hang on to it and publish it one day, when and if you wish.

Love,

Jim.[9]

Price made a brief annotation on the foot of the letter— ' "Autumn Testament" MS'—and sent Baxter a note acknowledging receipt of the work:

21 March, 1972

Mr James K. Baxter,
Jerusalem,
Private Bag,
<u>WANGANUI RIVER</u>

Dear Jim,

We are delighted to get *Autumn Testament*. I'll keep it by my bed to read, and be in touch soon.

Cheers,

<u>Hugh</u>[10]

Baxter and Price had first met in the early 1950s as students at Wellington Teachers' College. Between 1956 and 1958 they worked together producing school bulletins at the School Publications branch of the Department of Education. Price, who was a designer and artistic director, remembers frequently chasing Baxter up 'to ensure that publishing deadlines were met'.[11] By 1971 Price and his partner Bruce Milburn were well established as publishers, with offices in central Wellington. That same year, Baxter was back in Wellington for some months, following the winding-up of the first phase of the Jerusalem commune. For a time he lived among squatters in MacDonald Crescent. The squat was 'an old house near the centre of town. It was full of rubbish and inhabited by rats'.[12]

During this time Baxter became something of a fixture at the Price Milburn offices—always contriving to appear around morning-tea time. The staff enjoyed his company, however, so it was never a problem. One day he arrived with the manuscript of *Jerusalem Daybook*, which Price Milburn agreed to publish. Hugh Price discovered, while working on the project with Baxter, that although his appearance was scruffy—he was bearded, unwashed, unshod, and clad in op. shop clothes—when it came to editing his own work for publication, he was meticulous and focused.

Baxter was pleased with *Jerusalem Daybook*. By the time it was published he had returned to Jerusalem for the second phase of the commune:

Private Bag,
Jerusalem,
Wanganui River
29/2/72

Dear Hughie,
Me old mate, the book is a very finely produced job. Let me know how it sells. If it sells quickly—as it may—I think you could venture without worry on a reprint.
....
Yours till the roof falls in,
Hemi
(James K. Baxter)[13]

On 10 April Price Milburn forwarded the manuscript of *Autumn Testament* to the New Zealand Literary Fund Advisory Committee, requesting $375 to assist with the publication of the work.[14] The manuscript was undoubtedly safer with his publisher than with Baxter, although a second letter written on the same day indicated that for a few months longer it would maintain its rather precarious existence:

> I am enclosing the copy of *Jerusalem Daybook* which should have been included in the envelope posted today with our letter to you concerning a grant for the same author's new manuscript.
>
> Please note that the MS of *Autumn Testament* is the only one in existence, so it was posted to you, registered.[15]

On 28 August, less than two months before Baxter's death, 'the Minister of Internal Affairs, upon the recommendation of the Literary Fund Advisory Committee, … approved a grant of $300 … to assist in the publication of *Autumn Testament*'.[16]

In the context of his death, the title of Baxter's 'book of sorts' acquired a symbolic significance beyond his intention. What *Autumn Testament* might reasonably have implied—the articulation of a covenant worked out by a man at the height of his creative power—would be overshadowed by the legal connotations of a man in decay disposing of his property. Inevitably it was read as a presentiment of impending death and searched for clues that might explain his final days, as one might explore, for example, Keats' ode 'To Autumn'.

To those who seek such things, *Autumn Testament* obligingly appears to move towards closure. The review in the *Auckland Star* comments on the symmetry of bracketing the poem of the title with two shorter poems, 'one a love-song, the other a statement on Death and God, [which] are prologue and epilogue for the titlepiece'.[17]

The love-song—'He Waiata Mo Te Kare'—is Baxter's last and most moving verse letter to his wife. On the surface it attempts both to explain his decision to leave home for Jerusalem and to heal the hurt created. Yet its prevalent references to water recall earlier poems in which such imagery often implies confusion and ambivalence: the sea can symbolise death as well as regeneration; the wave-washed beach is a site of perpetual change; and the pond to which the 'Two ducks fly down/To…together' may offer sanctuary or stagnation.

The final poem in *Autumn Testament* is 'Te Whiori O Te Kuri'—'the tail of the dog/That wags at the end of my book'. It is a sonnet sequence, like the poem of the title, but with a tone at once reflective and weary. It is late autumn, and the world is redolent of decay: 'the kai falls from the trees', the statue of Te Whaea—the Mother of God—is 'eroded by moss', and Baxter expects to depart the 'lifelong grave of waiting'. When the poem's tail wags it sounds like the slow thump of an old dog sprawled on the hearth: 'it is possible to sit,/Light a cigarette, and rub/Your bruised heels on the cold grass'.

The forty-eight sonnets of the title poem come as close as anything Baxter has written to a last will and testament. As Baxter documents the life of the Jerusalem community, he anticipates its end. Its current members are often absent, its past ones mourned, and

> The darkness of oneself returns
> Now that the house is empty,
> …
> We who will certainly each of us one day return
>
> To our mother the grave. The darkness of oneself
> Comes from knowing nothing can be possessed.
>
> ('Autumn Testament', 6)

'Autumn Testament' anticipates Baxter's own end, but the characteristic imagery of death, often a disturbing feature of his poetry, now suggests peace and acceptance. Having taught himself to love spiders, he learns that 'Fear is the only enemy' and employs this knowledge to address the 'eight-eyed watcher/At the gate of the dead':

> … Therefore when I die,
>
> And you wait for my soul, you hefty as a king crab
> At the door of the underworld, let me pass in peace.
>
> ('Autumn Testament', 48)

The 'knowledge of death'[18] seems to inspire, in 'Autumn Testament', a revisitation of scenes and themes from Baxter's past. He had travelled a rocky road to get to Jerusalem. Most of his life he followed a double track, oscillating between the demands of correct society—where he played many roles—and his attraction to alienated tribes. He described his ancestors, Otago's early Scottish settlers, as the only tribe I know of ... their unfulfilled intention of charity, peace, and a survival that is more than self-preservation, burns like radium in the cells of my body; and perhaps a fragment of their intention is fulfilled in me, because of my works of art, the poems that are a permanent sign of contradiction in a world where the pound note and the lens of the analytical Western mind are the only things held sacred.[19]

Sonnet 14 recalls these origins and influences:

> Soon I will go South to my nephew's wedding
> To the quiet land I came from,
>
> Where all the ancestors are underground
> And my father now among them.

His father is also the link with a second, equally important, tribe: the pacifists of World War II. Baxter commented on the great 'difference between my own socialist–pacifist family and the semi-militarist activities of the people round about as the country moved towards war'.[20] Again in sonnet 14, he remembers the 'time when a Labour Government planted my brother/On the Hautu prison farm for five years/For walking in my father's footprint/And refusing to carry a gun'.

Other tribes followed: 'In two places I can find God without hindrance—before the Blessed Sacrament in a Catholic church; and at the heart of an [Alcoholics Anonymous] meeting, when the quiet, irresistible force of the Holy Spirit wells up in the hearts of those who are standing together on the same rock of reality.'[21] 'Autumn Testament' incorporates Baxter's last tribe, nga mokai—

'the fatherless'—into a mature expression of the integration of all his tribes within himself.

One of the key tensions in his life was between this attraction to the tribe and his participation in wider society. The 'family man, teetotal, moderately pious, not offensive to sight or smell, able to say the right thing in a drawing room' was ever at odds with the clannish, anarchic other self, 'my collaborator, my schizophrenic twin, who has always provided me with poems'.[22]

Baxter had developed at an early age this idea of himself as a composite figure. The schoolboy who 'would probably have replied in monosyllables or shown signs of apparent deficiency' was also a poet 'loath to expose my verse to the private or public eye'.[23] At the age of 17 he wrote a poem called 'Janus Unheard' in which he acknowledges the need to combine the two aspects of himself:

> Outside the rain is ceasing
>> Brilliant sunshine flashing in the rain;
> The rainbow represents the ancient covenant
>> And I must rear again
> My Janus-head out of a country coma
>> Of pastoral falsity[24]

'Janus Unheard' was inspired by Louis MacNeice's verse diary *Autumn Journal* (1939). Baxter admired MacNeice's 'amazing ability and subtlety within a limited scope' and found the 'insight into personality' pleasing.[25] In the search for influences on his later poetry the similarities between *Autumn Testament* and MacNeice's *Autumn Journal* (the least significant of which is the correspondence between titles) should not be overlooked. Both books move from recounting everyday occurrences in informal, colloquial tones to discussing weightier issues suggested by these commonplace events. In his early years Baxter had imitated MacNeice, and others, whose poems 'were giving voice to the social battles of our time'.[26] Three decades later *Autumn Testament* gives voice to similar struggles; the difference is that in Baxter's poetry authenticity has succeeded imitation.

Baxter's desire to amalgamate the two sides of his nature (his Janus faces) was best achieved at Jerusalem. The poems of this period express the synthesis of two selves that had always operated in tension. Baxter's early poems were the product of his experiences as the youngest son in a pacifist family during war. He would look back on these experiences as being

> in the long run very valuable, for they taught me to distrust mass opinion and sort out my own ideas; but at the time they were distinctly painful. I could compare them perhaps with the experiences of a Jewish boy growing up in an anti-Semitic neighbourhood. They created a gap in which the poems were able to grow.[27]

Tensions of this sort had become, for Baxter, a necessary condition for producing poetry. Always at the locus of tension was some version of the 'gap' between the selves, a paradoxical place where nothing existed but from which poems originated. In *Autumn Testament*, however, the gap becomes 'Wahi Ngaro: the void out of which all things come. That is my point of beginning. That is where I find my peace'.

The integration of the Janus faces was accelerated by Baxter's visit to India as a UNESCO fellow in 1958. Deprivation, which was little more than theoretical in New

Zealand, was painfully real in India. He was forever
changed by these first-hand experiences. In the opinion of
his wife, 'The road from India led to Jerusalem … What he
was trying to do later in Jerusalem was … still actually car-
ing for that kind of person.'[28] Baxter's biographer, Frank
McKay, makes reference to the images of the Indian poor
that 'were to linger in his mind for many years before being
memorably recalled in the Jerusalem books'.[29] In charac-
teristic fashion Baxter applies the lesson to New Zealand:

> This fine windy morning I think about
> The leper lying beside the fruitstalls in Calcutta
>
> Under the shade of the great bridge. The oil-stained
>   bandages
> Around his limbs, the flies moving slowly
>
> In and out of his nostrils,
>   …
> When he was younger he should have had a gun.
> There or in Karori, the sickness is, not to be wanted.
>
> ('Autumn Testament', 36)

From India Baxter moved inexorably towards Jerusalem
and 'the Lord on his axe-chopped cross'. On the way, po-
etry, which had for so long been the mainspring of his life,
became his own cross. His 1966–67 tenure as Burns Fellow
at Otago University was both the final, grand attempt to be
society's poet and the factor that tipped the balance
towards Jerusalem. He would later refer to it as 'a condi-
tional mistake … [That] hadn't exactly done me in but my
asbestos suit had worn through in a few places'.[30] By the
time the call to Jerusalem came he was primed to act on it:

... when I woke in the morning the first thought in my mind—was 'Jerusalem'—meaning not the city in Palestine, but the mission station on the Wanganui River. And either immediately or very shortly after a linked thought came into consciousness—that I should go to Jerusalem without money or books, there learn the spoken Maori from a man whom God would provide for me—whose name might or might not be Matiu—and then (God willing) proceed quietly and slowly to form the nucleus of a community where the people, both Maori and pakeha, would try to live without money or books, worship God and work on the land.[31]

One of the features of Baxter's decision to abandon his old life so ostentatiously was his commitment to stop writing poetry, an activity that now seemed at odds with his new vocation of poverty. Yet this was easier said than done for him. He could no more stop writing than he could stop breathing. The contradictions dogged him:

The man called James K. Baxter, who is like a dead body in the ground, swells up and gives off a stink of words. I suppose he does it for money and kudos.

It is absurd to say I am really a poor man while I keep on putting words together. Words set in order are mental possessions.[32]

His friend Colin Durning remembers saying to him, ' "I thought when you left you said no more books, no more poems" ... [He] looked at me and said, "Colin, I just can't help it ... [they] crawl up my back".'[33]

Baxter may have continued to write poetry, but he had little time for the niceties that accompanied the activity. He stopped keeping the notebooks he had filled so assiduously with poems since the age of 14 and seemed to discover a preference for publishers who could print his verse quickly.

The bibliographic room at Otago University was the first of these, although it was Durning who contracted them to publish the thirty-nine poems in *Jerusalem Sonnets: Poems for Colin Durning* (1970). The sonnets were something entirely new. Baxter had finally succeeded in discarding what he called the 'echo language … the twists of phrase (and so of thought also) that belonged by right to Hardy or Yeats or Dylan Thomas or Louis MacNeice'.[34] Bill Manhire points out that Baxter had so assimilated his influences that in the later work 'the process of absorption seems complete'. In the *Jerusalem Sonnets* Manhire recognises affinities only, not influences, and suggests that Lawrence Durrell is 'probably behind the unrhymed couplets'.[35] Baxter too credits Durrell's effect on his later verse, although more generally, with loosening 'up the chains of association, helping me to avoid heavy aphorisms about Time or God, and keep the eye on the invaluable sensory image'.[36]

In remarks on the *Jerusalem Sonnets* Vincent O'Sullivan fastens on the essence of Baxter's achievement in his last volumes:

There is no rhyme, no regularity of line length, no attempt, apart from an occasional inversion of word order, to do anything other than present simple speech in the loose iambics of normal spoken English. The sentences are often flat, the language almost ostentatiously matter of fact. The poems have taken on the very qualities of Baxter's own talk, its clarity and its care to avoid abstraction. They have the same tone of personal address, the same sudden flare of imagery. Imagery, in fact, is often the only 'effect' in much of the later poetry. It is the ordinary discourse of a man's chatting, reminiscing, explaining, and throughout it, quite as casually, the genius of his metaphor.[37]

Metaphor is the key to *Jerusalem Sonnets*, *Jerusalem Daybook* and *Autumn Testament*. In the two later volumes it becomes the agency whereby the prose passages obliquely gloss the poetry. In *Autumn Testament*, for example, Baxter elaborates, in his 'Letter to Colin', on his project to educate himself in the art of loving spiders—a metaphor for improvement through good works—that is one of the themes of the title poem. Having learned, by sonnet 48, how to say 'little Arachne, I love you', he confesses to Colin his 'savage joy' as he eradicates the spiders that spin their webs in the outdoor lavatory, 'spraying these two remarkable works of God, till they dangled by their forelegs and dropped down our bottomless pit'. Then in his imagination God, who has tired of Baxter's 'barren spirit', lets fly with his own 'great jet of Aerosol' and Baxter drops into Hell. Thus the prose gleefully subverts the poetry. By overlaying metaphor with metaphor Baxter reiterates a point first made in the notes to 'He Waiata Mo Te Kare', that, just as an arachnophobe does not invent a love for spiders, 'We do not create God by thinking about him'. *Autumn Testament*'s recurring thesis is that belief is the only way to Christ and that the essence of belief is faith. The real lesson to be learned from trying to love spiders is that there is no salvation through self-improvement. When faith alone exists, then the correct response springs 'out of the void of the heart'.

In many respects *Autumn Testament*'s most enthusiastic reviewers are correct. Baxter's last work synthesises the best features of *Jerusalem Sonnets* and *Jerusalem Daybook*. Its simplicity is the distilled essence of a life's writing, carrying the themes that were most significant, expressed in authenticity, shorn of imitation and derivation. In earlier works Baxter's tone might well be public and declamatory. In *Autumn Testament* the personal prevails:

> Both the girls are sick. I find it a drag
> To cook kai for the two of them,
>
> Ferry cups of tea, read some verse to Francie,
> Or carry a blanket for Siân—that's honest enough!
>
> I do it. It has its moments.
> I meant to go and rave down at Otaki
>
> Among the Catholic laymen, but this is more to
>   the point
>
>   ('Autumn Testament', 28)

In the humility of self-abnegating service Baxter learns to mock the brand of Franciscan poverty advertised in the earlier works. God's laughter no longer 'shakes the hills',[38] the poet alone is the butt of the joke:

> I think the Lord on his axe-chopped cross
> Is laughing as usual at my poems,
>
> My solemn metaphors, my ladder-climbing dreams,
> …
> … He has saddled me again
> With the cares of a household, and no doubt

Has kept me away from Otaki
Because I'd spout nonsense, and wear my poverty

As a coat of vanity.

('Autumn Testament', 29)

Grand symbols and big gestures lose significance when the end of poetry is unmediated communion between one man and his God.

Paul Millar

1 For a brief synopsis of the myths surrounding Baxter's death, and an account of the actual event, see William Broughton's notes, and Vonney Allan's story 'Hemi', in 'Vonney Allan's Account of James Baxter's Death', *Journal of New Zealand Literature*, 13 (1995): 285–90.

2 James K. Baxter, *Jerusalem Daybook* (Wellington: Price Milburn, 1971), p. 7.

3 James K. Baxter, *The Man on the Horse* (Dunedin: University of Otago Press, 1967), p. 122.

4 It was 'seized on' literally, going to numerous reprints and selling in the many thousands.

5 Peter Isaac, 'Baxter's Last Testament', *Sunday Times*, 26 Nov. 1972.

6 'J.K.' (Jack Kelliher), 'Last epistle of James K. Baxter', *Dominion*, 23 Dec. 1972.

7 C.K. Stead, 'Towards Jerusalem: The Later Poetry of James K. Baxter', *Islands*, 2.1 (1973): 7.

8 H. D. McNaughton, 'Baxter Affirms His Message', *Christchurch Press*, 27 Jan. 1973: 10.

9   James K. Baxter, letter to Hugh Price, undated, VUW Library, MS McKay item 5/82. Items held in the VUW Library are among the Baxter papers deposited by Dr Frank McKay.

10 Hugh Price, letter to James K. Baxter, 21 Mar. 1972, VUW Library, MS McKay item [5]/82.

11 Hugh Price, interview with Paul Millar, 26 May 1997.

12 James K. Baxter, introduction to *Notes on the Country I Live In* by Ans Westra (Wellington: Alistair Taylor, 1972), p. 6.

13 In private hands.

14 Price Milburn, letter to New Zealand Literary Fund Advisory Committee, 10 April 1972, VUW Library, MS McKay item 5/83/1.

15 Joan Smyth, letter to M. Jarman of the New Zealand Literary Fund Advisory Committee, 10 Apr. 1972, VUW Library, MS McKay item 5/83/2.

16 M. Jarman, New Zealand Literary Fund Advisory Committee, letter to Price Milburn, 28 Aug. 1972, VUW Library, MS McKay item 5/83/3.

17 'D.H.', review of *Autumn Testament*, *Auckland Star*, 6 Jan. 1973.

18 James K. Baxter, 'Conversation with an Ancestor', in *James K. Baxter as Critic*, ed. Frank McKay (Auckland: Heinemann, 1978), p. 113.

19 *The Man on the Horse*, p. 12.

20 *The Man on the Horse*, p 123.

21 James K. Baxter, *The Flowering Cross* (Dunedin: New Zealand Tablet, 1969), p. 33.

22 *The Man on the Horse*, p. 17.

23 James K. Baxter, letter to Noel Ginn, 12 Feb. 1943, VUW Library, MS McKay item 28/8.

24 James K. Baxter, 'Janus Unheard', Baxter Collection, Hocken Library, MS 704/12:709, p. 1.

25 James K. Baxter, letter to Noel Ginn, 10 Feb. 1944, VUW Library, MS McKay item 28/33.

26 James K. Baxter, 'Further Notes on New Zealand Poetry', Baxter Collection, Hocken Library, MS 975/119, p. 6.

27 *The Man on the Horse*, pp. 123–4.

28 Jacquie Baxter, interview with Bruce Morrison, 1996.

29 Frank McKay, *The Life of James K. Baxter* (Auckland: Oxford University Press, 1990), p. 170.

30 James K. Baxter, 'The Burns Fellowship', *Landfall* XXII (1968): 247.

31 *The Life of James K. Baxter*, p. 237.

32 James K. Baxter, *Jerusalem Daybook* (Wellington: Price Milburn, 1971), p. 17.

33 Colin Durning, interview with Bruce Morrison, 1996.

34 *Baxter as Critic*, p. 210.

35 Bill Manhire, 'Events & Editorials: Baxter's "Collected Poems" ', *Islands*, June (1981): 103.

36 *Baxter as Critic*, p. 210.

37 Vincent O'Sullivan, *James K. Baxter* (Wellington: Oxford University Press, 1976), pp. 42–3.

38 James K. Baxter, 'Poem for Colin—1', *Jerusalem Sonnets* (Wellington, Price Milburn, 1975), p. 9.

He Waiata
Mo Te Kare

1

Up here at the wharepuni
That star at the kitchen window
Mentions your name to me.

Clear and bright like running water
It glitters above the rim of the range,
You in Wellington,
I at Jerusalem,

Woman, it is my wish
Our bodies should be buried in the same grave.

2

To others my love is a plaited kono
Full or empty,
With chunks of riwai,
Meat that stuck to the stones.

To you my love is a pendant
Of inanga greenstone,
Too hard to bite,
Cut from a boulder underground.

You can put it in a box
Or wear it over your heart.

One day it will grow warm,
One day it will tremble like a bed of rushes
And say to you with a man's tongue,
'Taku ngakau ki a koe!'

3

I have seen at evening
Two ducks fly down
To a pond together.

The whirring of their wings
Reminded me of you.

4

At the end of our lives
Te Atua will take pity
On the two whom he divided.

To the tribe he will give
Much talking, te pia and a loaded hangi.

To you and me he will give
A whare by the seashore
Where you can look for crabs and kina
And I can watch the waves
And from time to time see your face
With no sadness,
Te Kare o Nga Wai.

5

No rafter paintings,
No grass-stalk panels,
No Maori mass,

Christ and his Mother
Are lively Italians
Leaning forward to bless,

No taniko band on her head,
No feather cloak on his shoulder,

No stairway to heaven,
No tears of the albatross.

Here at Jerusalem
After ninety years
Of bungled opportunities,
I prefer not to invite you
Into the pakeha church.

6

Waves wash on the beaches.
They leave a mark for only a minute.
Each grey hair in my beard
Is there because of a sin,

The mirror shows me
An old tuatara,
He porangi, he tutua,
Standing in his dusty coat.

I do not think you wanted
Some other man.

I have walked barefoot from the tail of
        the fish to the nose
To say these words.

7

Hilltop behind hilltop,
A mile of green pungas
In the grey afternoon
Bow their heads to the slanting spears of rain.

In the middle room of the wharepuni
Kat is playing the guitar,—
'Let it be! Let it be!'

Don brings home a goat draped round his
        shoulders.
Tonight we'll eat roasted liver.

One day, it is possible,
Hoani and Hilary might join me here,
Tired of the merry-go-round.

E hine, the door is open,
There's a space beside me.

8

Those we knew when we were young,
None of them have stayed together,
All their marriages battered down like trees
By the winds of a terrible century.

1 was a gloomy drunk.
You were a troubled woman.
Nobody would have given tuppence for our chances,
Yet our love did not turn to hate.

If you could fly this way, my bird,
One day before we both die,
I think you might find a branch to rest on.

I chose to live in a different way.

Today I cut the grass from the paths
With a new sickle,
Working till my hands were blistered.

I never wanted another wife.

9

Now I see you conquer age
As the prow of a canoe beats down
The plumes of Tangaroa.

You, straight-backed, a girl,
Your dark hair on your shoulders,
Lifting up our grandchild,

How you put them to shame,
All the flouncing girls!

Your face wears the marks of age
As a warrior his moko,
Double the beauty,
A soul like the great albatross

Who only nests in mid ocean
Under the eye of Te Ra.

You have broken the back of age.
I tremble to see it.

10

Taraiwa has sent us up a parcel of smoked eels
With skins like fine leather.
We steam them in the collander.
He tells us the heads are not for eating,

So I cut off two heads
And throw them out to Archibald,
The old tomcat. He growls as he eats
Simply because he's timid.

Earlier today I cut thistles
Under the trees in the graveyard,
And washed my hands afterwards,
Sprinkling the sickle with water.

That's the life I lead,
Simple as a stone,
And all that makes it less than good, Te Kare,
Is that you are not beside me.

Notes

Wahi Ngaro: the void out of which all things come. That is my point of beginning. That is where I find my peace.

When prayers, thoughts, desires, are bundled away in their necessary grave, it might seem that one has become an atheist. Trees are trees, hills are hills, men are men. There is no supernatural nimbus to tell us that God is present with and within his creation. Yet it is precisely then that the right thought, the right response, springs out of the void of the heart, and it is a 'prayer' to clean a drain or swear at some good friend. We do not create God by thinking about him.

Under the cold high stars here at Jerusalem it is not easy to recall the mood of rage and rock-bottom frustration that led me, in the town, to think for several months that I was becoming a Marxist. It is difficult to go back in spirit to that claustrophobic labyrinth. Yet all experience asks to be understood.

B— made a good comment this morning, referring to my stay at Macdonald Crescent. 'It must have been a very barren time for you, Hemi,' he said. 'But those experiences often turn out to be the most fruitful in the long run.'

He could be right.

Depersonalisation, centralisation, desacralisation: the three chief scourges of the urban culture. One has to look squarely at the Medusa's head that turns so many into stone before one can even begin to smile again. But one has to do it without anger. Otherwise the light of the Holy Spirit is excluded from one's meditation and dark-ness conquers the soul.

9

When I was in Wellington, F— rang me up. His fifteen-year-old daughter had vanished from home. He thought I might know where she was. I didn't know. He had travelled up from the South Island to look for her. She might have been in any one of a thousand flats.

'I don't intend to lock her in the cellar,' he explained. 'It's just that I want her to keep contact with us.'

He is an idealistic man and a good father. But the families can't fill the gap left by the broken communities. For years now, the headless growth of commerce and technology has been smashing down all the fences. The bill has to be paid, in death, crime, insanity, social dislocation. And men like F— are terrified of the anarchic society they have unintentionally helped to make.

I gave him a couple of addresses and suggested he should pray to God. The town flats, the borstal, the cabin of a coastal boat, even the morgue: she could be anywhere.

Anarchism, not anarchy, that is what I want. Then I could say to F—, 'Oh yes, your daughter is in the Y— Street community. She's not doing too badly. Go and see her there and have a yarn with her.'

★

Here at Jerusalem the blowflies pour into the kitchen and settle on the meat. When Keri had brought up a parcel of pork bones for us from the pa, the flies climbed under the paper and laid their clusters of eggs in every crevice. It was impossible to shut them out. We do not have the money to buy a fridge. I had to wash each piece of bone and meat separately under the tap before putting it in the pot.

The majority of the reporters are very like the blowflies. They add their own deposit of irrelevant half-truths to whatever is happening, and they do this for money. Reporters helped to pull down the original community here. If they come again, I think I'll say, 'There's nothing to report, brother. I'm here with my family. Do you want photographs of us adding milk to coffee? Do you want to come out to the lavatory and watch us shit?'

★

In the town, at my wife's place, the telephone rings continually. When I pick it up, I hear the voices of the drowning.

'Hemi, they've picked L— up on an I. and D. charge …'

'I can't believe in God …'

'Last night I cried and cried, and then I slashed my wrists …'

'I've got a habit on smack, and I want to get off it outside the hospital …'

'They won't let me keep my baby …'

'I need bread, Hemi. The Social Security buggers won't put me on the dole because I left the last job of my own accord. There's no jobs going and the fuzz are on my back …'

C— rings me up and tells me she is going mad again. I go out and visit her in her glass barn in the suburbs. She has what others have: a husband, three children and the telly.

'I was all right at Jerusalem,' she says. 'But here there's nobody. Nobody to see. Nobody to talk to.'

C— is a normal woman, I think. One day she will leave the glass barn and go to work, and move in the company of other people. She will not live at home. She will stay sane then. But from time to time she will dream that God is putting her in Hell for leaving her husband and children.

Be married and go mad; or be single and stay sane. The choice is Draconian. The problem is not lack of love. C— loves her husband and children. The problem is lack of community.

★

My son makes a Japanese bird out of paper. When you pull its tail, its wings flap.

'Don't you think it's a remarkable work of boredom?' he asks me.

My grand-daughter wants me to help her build a house with the hollow plastic bricks I gave her for her birthday. They are of three colours: yellow, blue and red. The letters of the alphabet are embossed on them. Each time we build a house she knocks it down and laughs.

★

My friend Tom is picked up by the police on an Auckland street for the double crime of being out of work and being Maori. It is the second crime that scandalises most the Catholic pakeha sergeant who arrests him. Escorted into the police station, Tom sits down on a chair and looks at the wall chart.

The sergeant kicks the chair out from under him. 'Don't look at that!' he shouts. 'Don't pretend you can read, you illiterate black shit! There should be a law to exterminate people like you.'

Tom feels very depressed. After he has spent a few days in Mount Eden on remand, he is released on bail. As we walk down the street together, he says to me, 'Man, I'd like to get some speed!'

'What the hell do you want speed for? It'll kill you quicker than smack.'

'In the town we need drugs as a shield.'

Tom is now in jail for two years on a drug charge. Who precisely is the criminal? Tom, for being out of work and for being Maori; the sergeant, for the misfortune of having been brought up in a traditional Catholic environment, with a wholly uneducated social conscience, apart from the usual steel-strong injunction not to masturbate and a racial prejudice as big as a house; myself, for worrying about both of them? Tame Hemahema used to tell me, 'If a dog worries, they shoot it.'

What I fear is Fascism under a different name, or very likely under no name at all. By a layman's definition, Fascism is atrocity accepted by all (except the victims) with the deepest equanimity. I think the seed of it is already with us.

★

In a rackrent house not far from Aro Street
  One dark morning
Four men sat with a bottle of wine at their feet,
  And the rain was falling.

The first man said, 'The Government's not my mother,
  I worked on the boats for twenty years
And all I've got to show for hard skippers and bad weather
  Is the price of five beers.'

The second man said, 'The screws and the magistrates
  Are wearing me down,
I've been in too many boobs and too many fights
  In too many towns.'

Then the third man said, 'I've not seen Jesus Christ,
    But if he came
To earth he should either have had a gun in his fist
    Or stopped the whole game.'

The fourth man reached for the bottle and said nothing
    But the light from the window
Showed like a graveyard lamp that his hands were shaking
    And his skin was like calico.

And the third man said, 'It will take more than talk
    To make this a country
Where the men who were treated like slaves will be
        able to work
    For other things than money.'

Then the four boobheads caught on the horns of the beast
    Saw on that dark morning
Above the town like lightning in the east
    The bones of Lenin shining.

I said to my wife Te Kare, 'I can't bring thirty people here.
And you can't shift into a community house.'
    'That's true,' she said. 'But I can put up one or two who
are sick. They need a place where they can rest.'
    Where she is, the water begins to flow from the rock.

    Oh early in the morning
    I wake up in Firetrap Castle
    Where the rats run free and the grots are smashed
    And the leaves grow thick at the window,

14

And first I light myself a smoke
With a mouth like old leather,
Then I put on my strides and a belt and a coat
To hold myself together,

And I go down to the Courtroom
To watch old Gabguts there
Riding with an iron saddle
On the backs of the poor,

For the fate of a boobhead is
That men do him bind
And plant him in the digger
Till he goes out of his mind,

And if you want to know more about it
Go and ask my friends
At the Duke or the George or the Bistro,
For the story never ends,

And the rich men pay the fuzz
And the fuzz arrest the poor,
And it's nothing new I'm saying to you,
It's all been said before,

And if you come by Firetrap Castle
Pay us a visit there,
But mind your head on the golden chandeliers
And watch out for the loose boards on the stairs.

Two jet planes fly over like gigantic metal birds. They
have their own beauty. I think I worship them. It would
not matter what Party or Power they belonged to, if they

scattered bombs down the length of this valley, I think one's soul would secretly acquiesce. Such energy and such precise destruction would seem just, simply because it was happening. There is nothing uncertain in their movement overhead.

> Then the pa children
> Run out to stare at
> The iron dove whose thunder
> Crucifies the spirit.

No doubt the cost of the fuel for a day's flight of one of these extraordinary machines could keep us in kai for a month. Is it necessary for them to fly? It is certainly necessary for us to eat.

I find myself able to withdraw that first temporary act of worship. Our century has made it plain that great machines are commonly controlled by uncharitable wills and limited minds. I remember what my father told me about his mother. When she saw the first aeroplane she had ever seen pass slowly overhead, she ran into her house, and cried out, 'It's the devil in his chariot !'

Two World Wars later, one might begin to see her point. Machines have not made us kinder or wiser. Do the means of destruction have to be so skilled and so immense? Christ was killed painfully and efficiently (pain being one purpose of that efficiency) on an ordinary wooden cross.

Autumn
Testament

1

As I come down the hill from Toro Poutini's house
My feet are sore, being bare, on the sharp stones

And that is a suitable penance. The dust of the pa road
Is cool, though, and I can see

The axe of the moon shift down behind the trees
Very slowly. The red light from the windows

Of the church has a ghostly look, and in
This place ghosts are real. The bees are humming loudly

In moonlight in their old hive above the church door
Where I go in to kneel, and come out to make my way

Uphill past a startled horse who plunges in the paddock
Above the nunnery. Now there are one or two

Of the tribe back in the big house—What would you
    have me do,
King Jesus? Your games with me have turned me into
    a boulder.

2

Wahi Ngaro, the void from which all life comes,
Has given us these woven spider-cages

That tie together the high heads of grass,
A civilisation in each. A stick can rip the white silk,

But that is not what I will do, having learnt
With manhood mercy, if no other good,

Two thousand perhaps in the tribe of nga mokai
Scattered like seeds now in the bins and the jails

Or occupied at their various occasions
Inside the spider-cage of a common dream,

Drugs, work, money. Siân, Kat,
Don and Francie, here with me at home

In the wharepuni—One great white flower
Shakes in the wind, turning a blind head towards
  our verandah.

3

Now we are short of meat, but up the path
Don comes carrying a goat on his shoulders

And I am astonished. 'What do you know,' he asks me,
'About butchering?' 'Not a bloody thing!'

Yet tonight I read a book by Debray the revolutionary
At the table where two candles burn

In front of the crucified Hero Father Theodore gave us,
While Don plays the guitar and Kat is talking

And Francie takes a bath in the other room,
And the dinner was good—half a goat's heart, a kidney
  and one testicle,

With cabbage and soya beans. Out on the hills
The moreporks are calling with human voices,

As the pa people tell us, for someone about to die,
But that could be anybody. Tonight we have our peace.

4

Wahi Ngaro, the gap from which our prayers
Fall back like the toetoe arrows

Children shoot upwards—Wahi Ngaro,
The limitless, the silent, the black night sky

From which the church huddles like a woman
On her hillock of ground—into your wide arms

Travelling, I forget the name of God,
Yet I can hear the flies roam through the rooms

Now at midday, feel the wind that flutters
The hippie goddess picture somebody painted

On an old blind and nailed on the wall. I can see
The orange flowers withering in a milk bottle,

Taste my tobacco phlegm, touch, if I like, the great
    bronze Christ
Theodore put up, on the poles of a cross he cut and
    bound himself.

5

Wahi Ngaro, now the ego like a sentry
At the gate of the soul closes its eyelids

For a moment, as today when
A crowd of ducks rose flapping at the place

Above the rapids where I go to bathe
Naked, splashing the water on my thighs,

And later I walked barefoot over the smooth boulders,
Thinking, 'There need be no other Heaven

'Than this world'—but rain spat soon
Out of a purple cloud, and I hid under

The willow leaves and bramble, as Adam did
Once from the Father. I brought back for Francie

A sprig of wet wild mint
That should go well tomorrow with the potatoes.

6

The darkness of oneself returns
Now that the house is empty,

A sense of danger in the room half dark,
Half lighted, seen through a squarish doorway,

Sticky rings left by cups on the table,
Darkness, the flutter of a moth,

A table spread in a tomb for the dead to eat at,—
That's it, the Dead!—'Why did you pay

'A visit to Toro at night? Night is the time for the
          morepork,'
Wehe told me today, as we sat down to

Fried Maori bread, meat and pickle,
We who will certainly each of us one day return

To our mother the grave. The darkness of oneself
Comes from knowing nothing can be possessed.

7

To wake up with a back sore from the hard mattress
In a borrowed sleeping bag

Lent me by Anne—it was her way, I think,
Of giving at the same time a daughter's

And a mother's embrace—friend, daughter, mother—
These kids have heart enough to nourish the dead world

Like David in his bed—to wake up and see
The sun, if not the light from behind the sun,

Glittering on the leaves beside the graveyard
Where some of them cleared the bramble and placed on
    the bare slab

A jam jar full of flowers—to wake is to lift up
Again on one's shoulder this curious world

Whose secret cannot be known by any of us
Until we enter Te Whiro's kingdom.

8

Brothers, the green walnuts are swelling
On the tree below the hill,

Round and hard, the shape of a man's scrotum,
And later on they'll fall in the grass

For us and the pa people. I sit in the transport shed
This morning of autumn, with the sun shining

And not a single cloud. Ria, Toro Poutini,
Talk about their many grandchildren,

And I say, 'Where I grew up in the South Island
There was a rock my father used to fish from;

'Sometimes he'd set a net in the channel of the rock
To catch—the sea is the one thing I miss

'Here up the River.' Poutini tells me then,
'You have the sea as well if you have this river.'

9

Groper with throats like buckets,
Lazy swimming greenbone,

The rippling bulk of the stingray,
The mother shark and her young ones,

Quartz-eyed barracouta,
The iron legs of the kina,

The tribes of the octopus,
Fat flesh of the tarakihi,

These images rise in sleep
Through the waters of my soul,—

As if I had been carried as a foetus
On the breast of Tangaroa,

And held in my heart an old hunger
To be dissolved and swallowed up by the waters.

10

The mossgrown haloed cross that crowns this church
Is too bleak for the mind of old Odysseus

Coming home to his table of rock, surviving and not
        surviving
Storms, words, axes, and the fingers of women,

Or the mind of Maui, who climbed inside the body
Of his ancestress and died there. Those who ride
        up river

In cars or the jetboat, see that high cross lifted
Above the low roofs of Jerusalem,

And speak of Mother Aubert and the Catholic Mission,
But when I see the sun fall and the moon rise

Over the edge of the ranges, I know what I have heard—
'The thoughts of a man's mind are many and secret'—

To the grass of the graveyard or a woman's breast
We turn in our pain for absolution.

11

At times when I walk beside the budding figtree
Or on the round stones by the river,

I meet the face of my dead father
With one or two white bristles on his chin

The safety razor missed. When he was younger
He'd hold the cut-throat with the ivory handle

And bring it with one deft stroke down his jowl,
Leaving the smooth blue skin. 'Old man,' I say,

'Long loved by me, still loved by many,
Is there a chance your son will ever join you

'In the kingdom of the summer stars?' He leaves me
Without a word, but like a touch behind him,

Greener the bulge of fruit among the figleaves,
Hotter the bright eye of the noonday sun.

12

The wish to climb a ladder to the loft
Of God dies hard in us. The angels Jacob saw

Were not himself. Bramble is what grows best
Out of this man-scarred earth, and I don't chop it back

Till the fruit have ripened. Yesterday I picked one
And it was bitter in my mouth,

And all the ladder-climbing game is rubbish
Like semen tugged away for no good purpose

Between the blanket and the bed. I heard once
A priest rehearse the cause of his vocation,

'To love God, to serve man.' The ladder-rungs did
      not lessen
An ounce of his damnation by loneliness,

And Satan whistles to me, 'You! You again,
Old dog! Have you come to drop more dung at Jerusalem?'

13

That grove of pines I prayed so long among
For the first six months, have been cut down for firewood

Or to make the floorboards of houses in the suburbs
Where children get square eyes. A dollar a hundred feet

Seems too small a price to get
For those green candelabra of the Ascension

Whose flames were pollen, but now the grove is gone
I go instead barefoot on the bulldozed clay,

Thinking, 'The pines are Pharisees,
They shove their solemn tough-barked crowns
       to Heaven

'But nothing grows under them.' One day on that
      ripped hill,
If God desires it, there will be a house

With Maori rafters, and over its doorway painted
      these words:
'Te Wairua o Te Kare o Nga Wai.'

14

Soon I will go South to my nephew's wedding
To the quiet land I came from,

Where all the ancestors are underground
And my father now among them. On my mother's wall

The picture Theo Schoon once painted
Shows him as the Iron Duke

With lines around his chin and mouth
Carved by the ploughshare. So he did look

In the time when a Labour Government planted
      my brother
On the Hautu prison farm for five years

For walking in my father's footprint
And refusing to carry a gun. Now in my mother's house

The picture is an icon. Father, is it easier to fight
The military machine, or the maggots of one's own heart?

15

The creek has to run muddy before it can run clear!
Here in this very room I have seen it happen,

The lads and the girls in chairs, some kneeling, some
    standing,
Some wearing headbands, one strumming the guitar,

And Father Theodore setting down an old
Packing case covered with a blanket

For the altar of his Mass. There was no wind
To burst the house door in, no tongues of fire,

But new skin under wounds, the Church becoming
    human,
As if religion were not the cemetery of hope

But a flowering branch—ah well, it was some time ago,
Sly is in jail under a two-year sentence,

Manu has gone back to the ward at Porirua,
And the Church can count her losses in Pharisaic peace.

16

Nobody can win that kind of battle,
I don't try it—for a month or two

At Macdonald Crescent it seemed we might be able
To twist the arm of the Public Works Department

And make them disgorge one old empty house,
But it came to nothing. The boys who sat for five hours
    in the Labour Bureau

And couldn't get the benefit, went to clink as usual
For being out of work. I tried the Ghandijian tactic

Of fasting on coffee and lemon juice
For twenty-five days. It didn't ruffle one single

Bureaucratic feather! With no grots, no light, no water,
We cooked our rice and spuds on the open fireplace

And remember the words of Saint John of the Cross:
'Our bed of love is made among the lions' dens.'

17

In those times the fast had made me thin
Though today the spare tyre is back under my belt,

And I'd go down for a coffee at the Hungry Horse
At three a.m. when the drunks gather,

And the dark angel of the town
Would mutter, 'Man, there's no way out

'Of this labyrinth! I mean to grind your soul
And theirs, and spit you out like rotten cabbage'—

Then Sharon at the corner with five sailors
Ran across to me and held my hand—

'Hemi, I'm going to crack it for ten bucks
With each of them; that way I'll get fifty;

'I'll hate it'—Above the town flickered the wings
Of the blood-red dove of Armageddon.

18

Father Lenin, you understood the moment
When the soul is split clean, as a man with an axe

Will split four posts from one log of dry timber,
But then your muzhiks still had souls

That smelt the holy bread upon the altar
And knew their mother's name. The mask of money

Hides too well the wound we cannot touch,
And guns are no use to a boy with a needle

Whose world is a shrinking dome of glass
A drug from Hong Kong will splinter open

With a charging elephant on a yellow packet
For riding home to deep sleep. The dollar is the point
    of it,

Old Father Lenin, and your bones in the Red Square
Are clothed in roubles till the Resurrection.

19

The bodies of the young are not the flower,
As some may imagine—it is the soul

Struggling in an iron net of terror
To become itself, to learn to love well,

To nourish the Other—when Mumma came from the bin
With scars from the wrist to the shoulder,

They combed her hair and put their arms around her
Till she began to blossom. The bread she baked for us

Was better kai than you'd get in a restaurant
Because her soul was in it. The bread we share in the
        churches

Contains a Christ nailed up in solitude,
And all our pain is to be crystal vases,

As if the mice were afraid of God the cat
Who'd plunge them into Hell for touching one another.

20

Somebody in my dream was shaking a blanket
Sending a gust of wind with dust and fleas

Over my body—and when I woke,
In the dark room I saw a wavering shape

Like a vampire in a castle in the stories
I used to read as a boy. Whether or not it came

From the graveyard forty feet away
From the house corner, fear increases the strength

Of any kehua—so I crossed over and switched on the light,
Smoked a cigarette, chewed over a few pages

Of Peter Marin, and began to write this poem,
Since a man who'll die some day should hardly fear
    the dead,

And the tribe need a father who is afraid only
Of ceasing to love them well.

21

King Jesus, after a day or a week of bitching
I come back always to your bread and salt,

Because no other man, no other God,
Suffered our pains with us minute by minute

And asked us to die with him. Not even guilty,
This morning I say the Salve Regina

While the fog is shifting slowly out of the trees,
Fry four slices of bread and eat them,

Then sit down under the image that stood once
In a Dutch farmhouse, then in a room in Putaruru,

Now in this place. It is perhaps the nimbus
Of Theodore's thick body and solar heart

That clings to the bronze, bringing to mind
Abundant loaves and multiplying fishes.

22

To pray for an easy heart is no prayer at all
Because the heart itself is the creaking bridge

On which we cross these Himalayan gorges
From bluff to bluff. To sweat out the soul's blood

Midnight after midnight is the ministry of Jacob,
And Jacob will be healed. This body that shivers

In the foggy cold, tasting the sour fat,
Was made to hang like a sack on its thief's cross,

Counting it better than bread to say the words
        of Christ,
'Eli! Eli!' The Church will be shaken like a

Blanket in the wind, and we are the fleas that fall
To the ground for the dirt to cover. Brother thief,

You who are lodged in my ribcage, do not rail at
The only gate we have to paradise.

23

The heat moves into my bones again
Here on the edge of the verandah

Father Te Awhitu mended hour by hour
With new boards where the rain had rotted them

Pouring down from a roof that has no spouting,
And when I asked him why, replied, 'Mahi mo Te
        Atua'—

'Work done for God'—the day the house was ready
I lit the stove in the front room,

That cost me twenty dollars secondhand in Wanganui
And had a broken lid—wood, stove, matches,

The first flame rising—so the house became
Inhabited with the flame of non-possession

That burns now and always in the heart of the tribe,
Too simple a thing for the world to understand.

24

The brown grass that Barry cut for us
With the new sickle, is lying in heaps

Between the house and the door of the pataka
Where we stuck our mattresses. Barry has gone

Perhaps to Oakley where they'll pump him full of drugs
And ask him the meaning of the tattoos on his arm—

'Dad; Love; Hate'—he used to sail like a swan
Through the middle of the Courtroom up to the dock,

His coat split above his buttocks,
Boots loud on the floor, his forelock hanging

Over one eye, then tossed back, a debutante
Under the gaze of his friends. The fuzz were

Ignorant lovers in that brain-smashing courtship
Where love words are swearwords and kisses are blows.

25

Richard will not come here, the shy one,
Wary as a crayfish whose feelers jut out

From a crevice in the rock. When he was thirteen,
In the maths class, his teacher used to stand him

In a wastepaper basket at the front of the room,
And once I heard the lawyer ask him,

'Can't you think of something better to do with
        your life?'
'No.' The face like a young stone mask:

'Idiots have no opinions.'
I heard him breaking bottles in the street

The night Naomi turned him down;
Naomi was a mother who had found him

Too hard to carry. Yet he broke no windows.
It hurts me to watch the snaring of the unicorn.

26

I go up the road under the eye of Te Ra,
And a cicada flying gets tangled in my hair

Until I set him free. Just as I finish
The Mystery of the Crowning with Thorns,

Rex pulls up in his truck—'The new overseer
Is a little Hitler … The gristle's gone from my hipbone,

'When I lie down in bed the bones pull
Out of their socket.' He drives on through the dust.

I keep him in mind through the Carrying of the Cross,
Then kneel for God's Death by the black plastic tank

Where troughs are stuck in the moss to catch
The meagre trickle of midsummer

That flows through the pipe to the house. It's cool
    up here
Under the green ribbed branches of the pungas.

27

When I stayed those three months at Macdonald Crescent
In the house of Lazarus, three tribes were living

In each of the storeys—on the ground floor, the drunks
Who came there when the White Lodge burnt down;

Above them, the boobheads; and scattered between
    the first
And second storey, the students who hoped to crack

The rock of education. The drunks are my own tribe.
One Sunday, the pubs being shut, they held a parliament

In the big front room—Lofty with his walking stick,
Phil the weeper, Taffy who never spoke much,

And one or two others—in conclave they sat, like
    granite columns
Their necks, like Tritons their faces,

Like tree-roots their bodies. Sober as Rhadamanthus
They judged the town and found it had already
    been judged.

28

Both the girls are sick. I find it a drag
To cook kai for the two of them,

Ferry cups of tea, read some verse to Francie,
Or carry a blanket for Siân—that's honest enough!

I do it. It has its moments.
I meant to go and rave down at Otaki

Among the Catholic laymen, but this is more to
        the point
With Kat and Don away. Francie becomes active,

Sleeps in draughts, wanders through the house,
Siân lies quiet in a Buddhist cloud

Of 'flu bugs and vegetarian torpor,
A girl from the Welsh hills. The mood of family

Soon takes over, and they become my daughters,
I their Granpop. We get to know each other well.

29

I think the Lord on his axe-chopped cross
Is laughing as usual at my poems,

My solemn metaphors, my ladder-climbing dreams,
For he himself is incurably domestic,

A family man who never lifted a sword,
An only son with a difficult mother,

If you understand my thought. He has saddled
        me again
With the cares of a household, and no doubt

Has kept me away from Otaki
Because I'd spout nonsense, and wear my poverty

As a coat of vanity. Down at the Mass
Today, as Francie told me to, I took Communion

For her (and Siân as well) cursing gently
The Joker who won't let me shuffle my own pack.

30

Simply for bowing one's head in a little matter,
Strange that so great a peace should come!

I find that the flower like a star beside the power pole
Is made up of thirty separate flower-heads,

Each one a different blossom—why, I can't say,
But the light of God shines out of them,

The delicate pure invisible light I have not
Seen since I left Grafton. In those days

I'd climb the hill on the Domain
Before dawn, when the leaves were cold as iron

Underfoot, and talk with the trees—this one
Thinking she was ugly in her narrow dress of bark,

That one a woman who'd had many children—
The tree nymphs—their great beauty made me tremble.

31

I tell the girls, 'After long meditation,
Scrutiny of books in Arabic and Latin,

'Consultation (by telephone) with twenty-five colleagues,
Examination with bioscope and xylophone,

'I have come to the crux of my diagnosis,
Your ailment is a hybrid,

'Tuberculosis, cholera, leprosy,
In one package'—they are not impressed,

Nor, I think, is the master of the house,
The Maori sergeant from the First World War

In uniform, seated on a cane chair
In the foot-high photograph upon our mantelpiece.

I think he has summed us up—'Kaore nga pukapuka!
You might stay well if you learnt Maoritanga.'

32

Life can be a hassle. Are you free of it, Monsignor,
While you dispute the changes of the liturgy

Or polish up your golf style? At one p.m.
Either in your house or my house

The soul may plunge into pain like a child who slides
Through the grass at the lip of a mine-shaft,

Therefore don't ask me, 'What do you mean by that
    statement
You made to the Weekly News?'—or—'What precisely is

Your relation to Sally X—?' A man is a bubble
Sticking to the edge of a mighty big drainpipe!

Let us be content to play one game of chess,
Share a coffee and biscuit, let Christ work out
    the deficit,—

There were eight souls, they say, with Father Noah;
Neither you nor I might have made it to the
     gangplank.

33

'Mother, your statue by the convent path
Has chips of plaster scattered round it

'Where rain or frost have stripped you of your
     mantle—'
'It doesn't matter.' 'As you know, in winter

'I often kneel there under the knife-edged moon
Praying for—' 'I hear those prayers.'

'Mother, your blue gown seems like stone,
Too rigid—' 'What they make of me

'Is never what I am.' 'Our Church looks to the young
Like a Medusa; they want to be—'

'Free, yes; Christ is the only Master.'
'They are taught to judge themselves.' 'Suffer it.'

'But sin—' 'I see no sin. My secret is
I hold the Child I was given to hold.'

34

At evening the sandflies would rise from the river
And bite our bare ankles where we waited

For a tug on the line. Peter had dug
A pit in the bank to throw the eels in,

And when we caught one he tossed it there
To twist like a snake, the slime on its body

Plastered with mud. 'Hemi, pray for a catch.'
'It's quiet on the water;

'God is here.' We caught two more,
And took the first one up to Koro Rangi

In case he wanted a kai. One eel fed twelve people,
But Peter was a chef. Carl put five eels in the bath

And studied them with an elf's attention,
The way their fins moved, the way they intertwined.

35

The stove will blaze here in the winter
Heating the whole room. We still need

Blankets, money for kai, money for lighting,
Stones laid on the path between the house and the cottage,

New iron and paint for the roof, some window glass,
Five or six chairs, two doors, a fridge for the meat,

A verandah beam and spouting—Good to be poor!
Without God our boat will sink,

And that is the way it should be. The blind man hoisted
The lame man on his back, and then the blind man

Had eyes, the lame man, legs. By his old habit,
I'd say, God will let us wait till the boat is sinking

Then bail it out in a minute. Still that man goes
Walking on the water and thinking his own thoughts.

36

This fine windy morning I think about
The leper lying beside the fruitstalls in Calcutta

Under the shade of the great bridge. The oil-stained
     bandages
Around his limbs, the flies moving slowly

In and out of his nostrils, over his eyelids;
That lion face of dark mahogany

Turned up its brow to the overlying cloud
Behind which Rahm might live, from which a
     few spots

Of rain aspersed the pavement. I threw some coins
Into his tin dish. The policeman, built like a Maori,

Guarding the fruitstalls in his khaki shorts,
Said, 'They're no use to him.' But the man was not
     quite dead.

When he was younger he should have had a gun.
There or in Karori, the sickness is, not to be wanted.

37

I have seen them play the guitar round the bonfire
Out there on the grass, night after night,

With a little beer and a few roast potatoes,
But now the tribe has gone. Ella, Warwick,

Abe, Red Steve, Moth, Belligerent Mike,
And fifty others—when I meet them on the pavements

Their heads hang down, the mask is back again
By which the town holds itself together,

But here they needed no mask. Abe, with one lung
Deflated, would wheeze all night like a blowhole

Behind a curtain in the top bunk,
But I saw him with a shovel in the bottom of the pit

They dug for the shithouse, tossing earth to the sky,
His dark face wrinkled with the tribal smile.

38

Last night a grey nimbus round the moon,
Today the rain comes from the west;

The leaves on all the trees look greener,
Rangimotu is burning piles of dry grass in his garden,

The flames go up to the low heaven,
And Wehe shouts to him from the door of her kitchen,

'You, come in out of the rain!' He only smiles
And goes on raking. I carry up the hill

A milk bottle full of sauce, bread and a parcel of sausages;
I plug the jug in and wait for it to boil

While the girls lie in bed. 'I like the rain.'
'I like it too. Aren't you afraid, Hemi,

'Of catching the 'flu?' 'Not exactly.
It's only that—' The rain comes down in a dense
        white curtain.

39

The centre of our dreaming is the cave
That the world translates as brothel. Margaret told
    me once

A dream she had, about a house
In a meadow by the sea, old and full of passages,

Upstair and downstair rooms where the tribe were sleeping,
And three great waves came out of the sea

And washed around the house and left it standing,
Though for a while they had hidden the sun and the
    moon.

There has to be, I think, some shelter,
A home, an all-but-God, an all-but-mother

In time and place, not just the abstract void
Of I looking for me. Around these walls

They dipped their hands in paint and left their handprints
As on the walls of caves the Magdalenian hunters.

40

Three tourists come out of the church and stand on the
    grass rim
Above the pa. One of them points

At the big hall roofed with new iron
And walled with plaster board, where the men who
    built the bridge

Cooked their meals and slept at night—
'That's where the hippies lived. They had to kick
        them out.'

'They couldn't do much harm in this place.'
Their eyes are lenses looking at the houses,

Five or six, two of them windowless,
And missing out the aroha. Their fantasies will never

Be shifted in a world that's built to turn
On Us and Them. An old fear grips my belly

When I hear the brassed-off voices of the executioners
Who may one day come to burn us out of our burrow.

41

Twenty buckets of water for the bath,
And then another seven or so

Because it's too hot. 'Thank you, Hemi,'
Francie lisps in the small-child voice

She uses as one mask among a dozen,
But that is her privilege. She has not yet got over

The fire-walking ceremony of the Plymouth
        Brethren
And maybe never will. We each have

Our necessary games. But at this house
Where all things hang from moss-bearded branches

The hernias of the mind retract themselves
Month by month. The ones who used to come here

Like divers to a decompression chamber
Staggering, won't come again. I have to say, 'So be it.'

42

The rata blooms explode, the bow-legged tomcat
Follows me up the track, nipping at my ankle,

The clematis spreads her trumpet, the grassheads rattle
Ripely, drily, and all this

In fidelity to death. Today when Father Te Awhitu
Put on the black gown with the silver cross,

It was the same story. The hard rind of the ego
Won't ever crack except to the teeth of Te Whiro,

That thin man who'll eat the stars. I can't say
It pleases me. In the corner I can hear now

The high whining of a mason fly
Who carries the spiders home to his house

As refrigerated meat. 'You bugger off,' he tells me,
'Your Christianity won't put an end to death.'

43

On the willows Don has felled by Poutini's cottage
The leaves are heavy with reddish galls,

Lumps like oval cysts, and if you break them open
You find inside a pale thin grub

Arching its body. When I came up from the town
My feet had spreading lumps that filled with fluid,

Hard as an egg and larger than a finger,
Got by walking on the roasting asphalt

Below Macdonald Crescent. The life of the streets dug in,
Taking charge. I thought my feet were rotting.

Keri brought me some strips of bark his father
Had cut in the hills. I boiled the bark for half an hour,

Poured that water into a plastic tub
And soaked my feet. In two days the lumps were gone.

44

This testament, a thing of rags and patches,
Will end soon. I cannot say, like Villon,

'Pray for me and for yourselves,'
For this is another century. That poor man ate
    his lunch

With the corpses of streetboys hanging overhead
And was part owner of some kind of brothel,

But the harps and lutes of paradise on the church wall
Were just as real as the bogs of fire,

The burghers sweated in their high fur gowns,
The slaves lay down to sleep on a straw mattress,

And most of it made sense. As if God had opened
A crack in the rock of the world to let some daylight in,

Saying, 'Be poor like Me.' Our life is the one
We make in darkness for ourselves.

45

Tomorrow I'll go down to Wellington,
Hitching, if I'm lucky, a ride down the river road

Past the karaka trees and the town houses
That turn the river into the Wanganui ditch

With shit that floats upstream below the bridges
When the tide pushes home. I'll go then

Southward among the sad green farms
Where the sheep get more freedom than their
      masters,

Past beaches with the plumes of toetoe blowing
In a wind that only Maori kids on horses

Can bargain with, down, down the straight coast road
To the dream city, the old fat sow

Who smothers her children. I'll wear no diving suit
And sit cross-legged in a pub doorway.

46

After writing for an hour in the presbytery
I visit the church, that dark loft of God,

And make my way uphill. The grass is soaking my
      trousers,
The night dark, the rain falling out of the night,

And the old fears walk side by side with me,
Either the heavy thump of an apple

Hitting the ground, or the creaking of the trees,
Or the presence of two graveyards,

The new one at the house, the old one on the hill
That I have never entered. Heaven is light

And Hell is darkness, so the Christmen say,
But this dark is the belly of the whale

In which I, Jonah, have to make my journey
Till the fear has gone. Fear is the only enemy.

47

On the scrim of the walls the tribe have written up—
'You're all freaks'—'Men only'—

'Humpers Unite'—'Blessed are the peacemakers'—
'The slowest beasts are strongest and live the longest'—

'This is the tumour on Jo's brain'—
'Fuck War'—'The Mighty Merkin'—

'Love is like nothing else but love'—
'A simple, goodly person called Mumma lived here'—

The chorus of their chaos becomes a possible Christ
When the light behind the face begins to shine,

Who wear no shoes in the street because
Rain was invented to kiss the feet of the poor.

I go south tomorrow with the river
And leave no lock on my door.

The spider crouching on the ledge above the sink
Resembles the tantric goddess,

At least as the Stone Age people saw her
And carved her on their dolmens. Therefore I don't
      kill her,

Though indeed there is a simpler reason,
Because she is small. Kehua, vampire, eight-eyed watcher

At the gate of the dead, little Arachne, I love you,
Though you hang your cobwebs up like dirty silk in
      the hall

And scuttle under the mattress. Remember I spared your
      children
In their cage of white cloth you made as an aerial castle,

And you yourself, today, on the window ledge.
Fear is the only enemy. Therefore when I die,

And you wait for my soul, you hefty as a king crab
At the door of the underworld, let me pass in peace.

Letter to Colin

They are building a hinaki out of wire in the middle room tonight. I think it will be successful. It is about eight feet long—or looks so, from this end of the table—and the entrance funnel for the eels is promisingly small. Taraiwa told us last night that the funnel opening should face downstream, because the eels smell the bait and move upstream to get at it, but are not intelligent enough to do more than nose around the end of the hinaki that faces towards them, if it is the end that has a lid on it.

I get up from my sleeping bag to write this note. The family have gone to bed. It is after midnight. The tensions in my body (a legacy from alcoholism to which I am well used) will not allow me to sleep. It is a good time for writing.

My family are hard-working these days. They have built a large strong hen-run and coop for the two hens and rooster we have had sent up from Wanganui. They have painted it red. There seems to be some danger that the rooster may have taken monastic vows. So far he has shown no interest in his two wives, apart from some short union discussions about the superfluity of vegetable scraps and the absence of wheat. A pity. We could do with some fertilised eggs for them to hatch into chickens.

I have agreed with the house-owner, Mrs Winterburn, to keep the number of the family down to ten. She rang us up the other day, disturbed because she had heard rumours that I was re-opening the original open-door community. I can't blame her for feeling worried. She and her sisters have had to put up with endless unwelcome publicity and criticism, so prolonged that it looks at times like the work of te taipo. As you know well, Colin, by visiting us, nine-tenths of what the papers said about us was nonsense, and the other

51

tenth came from the inevitable problems of overcrowding if you decide not to turn people away.

It is not possible for us to re-open the community. No doubt it served its purpose. I accept the present arrangement as the will of God. We owe a great debt to Mrs Winterburn and her sisters. I do not intend to lay another boulder on their backs.

This way it is more peaceful for us too. We are a cheerful family. It does hurt me at times to send visitors on their way. They go back so often to a labyrinth from which there is no apparent exit. But I am learning to leave such matters to Te Atua. Undoubtedly, when the open-door community was here, the house was often overcrowded, the sense of Maoritanga was frequently cloudy, and it was hard to get work done. Mahi was the little finger on our hand. Now it has begun to grow. Two of my family are carpenters, and the girls keep the house clean, mopping it out with water and disinfectant daily. In the family we have a good balance of Maori and pakeha members.

I have fallen away from the Franciscan spirit. The other morning I took a tin of fly-spray and sprayed the two gigantic spiders who had long been roosting at the back of our outdoor lavatory. They used to sit there at the door of their private tunnel, legs and jaws ready for action, among carefully constructed platforms and fly-traps of web, apparently in a state of connubial concord. The female showed no signs of eating the male. Perhaps they had been affected by our atmosphere of family peace.

Recently I had been training myself to love spiders. But I confess I took a savage joy in spraying these two remarkable works of God, till they dangled by their forelegs and dropped down our bottomless pit. There has been a spiritual backlash. My imagination tells me that one day God, tired of my barren spirit, will spray me with a great jet of Aerosol, and leave me to drop into Hell. But I have to remember he is merciful to his unmerciful creatures.

When I met you at Port Chalmers, I would have liked to stay with you. After leaving the Varsity job, and losing the borstal job, I knew you were travelling in a gap of uncertainty where no one can be fully at peace. Yet I felt peace in your company. It is often like that. Here too I have my own variety of suffering. There are wounds in my soul which God probably means to leave open. But those who come here always comment on the peace of the place, and indeed we are at peace. Peace and pain are often intimately connected.

My conscience accused me this morning, after breakfast, because for a few minutes I had it in mind to keep for myself the last packet of family cigarettes, which Steve had brought out from the cupboard in the pataka. I repented, Colin, but it was a severe breach of the spirit of poverty. I gave the packet to another member of the family, the least certain of himself, and told him to take one and put the packet on the table where everybody would be able to help themselves.

To kill a spider; to keep cigarettes for one's own use; to worry about food bills; to lie awake and feel discouraged by the auto-erotic tensions of an ageing body—these are my sins, and very likely no priest in his right mind would take much notice of them. But they reveal, as usual, an unconscious egoism which only God can cure. I come here to give him the opportunity to cure it.

In myself what is not myself, the rind of a lifelong ego-ism, is an obstacle to his mercy. His mercy is perfectly signified by the sun and the calm autumn trees loaded with fruit and the great cliff of treeferns that rises mound after mound behind this house. The maternal richness of nature is part of the redemptive equation which our mea-suring, grabbing mind can never grasp.

At Hiruharama we go beyond the conscious shell of knowledge, that part of the soul which says—'I want; I have; I am'— into the darkness of the anima, the yin prin-ciple in the mind which may be compared to the night itself. It is necessary to make this journey. The anima is the area familiar to Maori thought, the place of fear, the passive night from which dreams come, where one encounters the spirits of nature and the spirits of the dead. At times the journey may be agonising. It may demand the last ounce of oneself, to go beyond oneself, to walk the waters of availability to all things and all persons. But there is always peace beyond the agony. We wait to be turned into entire creatures. At the centre of the darkness we wait for the light of the spiritus to shine, the light that the disciples saw on the Mountain of Trans-figuration.

I go to Auckland soon for a day or two. May God bless you and keep you. Pray for us. Our boat is small. I would like to see other boats set floating. There are so many people drowning. The towns are becoming intolerable to me. I cannot stay in them long without beginning to ask for the help of Father Lenin. But perhaps God sees a value in the smoky passages of that burning house out of which his mercy delivers us. My greatest dread is that one day he may ask me to go back and live in comfort.

I embrace you.

★

Some of the local people are not entirely happy with my recently published Daybook. I say to them, 'I've tried not to hang out anybody's washing.'

'The swear words you have in the book should not be there.'

'If you're making porridge,' I reply, 'you need some salt. A man can put in too much salt or too little. I didn't think I'd put in too much.'

Not all of them are convinced. Perhaps I should say, 'When you put a hinaki in the water, you don't use fresh meat for a bait inside it. You wait till the meat smells a bit. Then you catch many tuna.'

Or else—'If you eat the fresh karaka berries they will poison you. But if you boil them for a few hours, then you can eat them.'

In a sense I agree with the people. To write a book is always to do some harm. There are far too many books in the world. And any child, or person not used to different styles of writing, can pick up a book and be shocked or worried by it. Yet I do not think the harm done by an honest book will lead to the death of anyone's soul. Honesty is like an axe. No doubt it hurts the wood to be turned into posts and strainers.

Politeness is a different thing from courtesy. Politeness may come from fear. Courtesy always comes from love. A courteous man may swear at his friend either to make a strong point or to put him at ease. Yet to stick the words

55

down in a book is another matter, I know. Perhaps all the books I write are like letters to friends, and I would prefer those who don't understand them to put them quietly down again.

I think Te Atua wanted me to write the book just as I wrote it. But he would know that some suffering would come from it. The suffering that comes to myself I should learn to welcome. The suffering that comes to others I should regret. Yet suffering seems to be a side effect of any action.

★

On the second Sunday of Lent Father Te Awhitu gives us a brief sermon about the Transfiguration. 'I think it was like Heaven,' he says. 'They were up the mountain, nobody else there, with Our Lord and Moses and Elias. It was like in a family. Our Lord told them not to speak about it. You don't talk about what happens in a family to everybody.'

He also says, 'Peter wanted to make houses, for Our Lord and for Moses and for Elias.' And—'They adored Him.'

This sermon sheds more light than many books. I had never understood Peter's wish to make arbours out of leaves. It would come from a memory of the Jewish ceremony where the people made tents of leaves in the courtyards, and it would also be the natural thought of a poor man on a journey, to make a shelter for those whom he served and loved. To make huts in Heaven.

I speak myself, as Father Te Awhitu has asked me to, about prayer, but to less effect. Last week I compared Our Lord to the Wharepuni, which is the body of the ancestor sheltering the tribe with his arms and ribs.

Te Atua sends me a good instructor in Father Te Awhitu. His few words have the weight of wedges splitting timber. His soul speaks of God because it is at rest in God.

Te Huinga comes to me, and speaks of the inertness of spirit she finds burdensome in herself. She says, 'I cannot believe, Hemi.'

I say, 'Your soul is like the earth. It has a lot of strength. But your pains will be slow to shift and the joy slow to come. It is like a woman waiting nine months for a child to be born.

'God will give each of us a white stone at the end of the world. The secret name of each of us will be written there, the name he gives us, and only the man himself will be able to read it. I can't tell what your name will be. But I think in my own mind it will be "Mercy"—not just the mercy he shows to you, but the mercy as well that you show to others.'

Her face shines with love. I suppose these are the times of transfiguration that should not be mentioned outside the family. There are many of them. But the world would see only our bare feet and old clothes.

Tonight again Te Atua presses heavy on me. He will not let me sleep. I itch all over, but not from insects. The griefs of the tribe have communicated themselves to me—six of them had their difficulties to be resolved before and after midnight, and when I embraced them, I think, as often happens, their tensions flowed into me as electricity flows into the wire that conducts it to the ground. My muscles ache and my body is cold.

In the darkness before dawn I put on my coat. I go outside to urinate. The stars are pure and high and the moon is going down behind the big poplar. The beauty of his night shames me. My praise cannot rise as high as his Heaven. I want, not his pain, not his cold, but the peace-giving friendship and the ointment of welcome of Father Eugene in Auckland. There I will sleep like a child.

He does not want us always to be children. I had forgotten it is Lent, though I said at Mass yesterday—'Ko te mahi mo tenei Reneti, ko nga karakia.' Instead of praying, I write to you.

Te Ariki tells us—'What sorrow is like my sorrow?' If it were incommunicable, though, he would not express it to us. His sorrow is both ours and not ours. It is beyond us, yet spears slide out of it to pierce our little hearts. I say to him, 'Let me have your sorrow,' but probably I am insincere. I love him, yet his sorrow terrifies me. To go into it, out of the warmth of the tribe, is too like dying before death.

Come gently to me, Ariki rite ki Te Ra, I am not used to your pain, I have to learn to bear it by degrees. You are the heart of every heart and the meaning of all meaning. To die in your company is better than to be brought to Heaven. If I wince and complain every hour of my life, it is not me but my idiot brother, my second self. He tino pai te mate. This is the only place where I can be I, by being not I but the other I was born to be.

Kua mutu. Kaore. Kua ara te ra o nga tangata. Kua ara Te Ariki rite ki Te Ra.

I could be happy if I had no evil dreams. In the bog of my dreams I suffer whatever I have been or could be, whatever is exiled from the peace and love and simple activity of this house. I am scattered among corpses and demons. I am tossed up and down like a leaf on a black wind. Yet this may mean no more than that my soul is open to the world we live in. What right has a man to peace in the century of Hiroshima? Or when in his own country men and women go mad daily because they can see no sense in the lives they live and the deaths they are going to die? The doctrine of original sin is the most peace-giving of Christian doctrines. To name the incubus is also to recognise that we share the burden in common with all men. That is to take the first step on the road of liberation.

Tom Hepi is dead now. In his son's house at Taumarunui I had a dream. I was back in Auckland. Great heaps of rags and rubbish, tarry with filth, like ancient hospital bandages, were burning in the streets, on iron brackets, and men in greasy clothes were tending the fires. The smoke blew through the town, through the otherwise empty squares, among buildings of high concrete with windows like blank eyes. The wind came from the horizon, over the harbour, under a lid of cloud, as if from the space behind the stars.

The wind overturned one of the rusty brackets and sent it spinning in my direction, bashing against the walls of the buildings like a huge bird. I had the sense of panic that comes from life out of control. The pain of sharing the world's evil, of being a leper in a city of lepers—this clung to me like the drifting smoke.

I think it was a dream of Gehenna. A true dream. The valley of Gehenna was the rubbish dump of Jerusalem. They tipped out there everything they had no use for, and the fires burned night and day.

The wind is the Holy Spirit blowing in Gehenna. The fire is the fire of the Divine Love consuming our hearts. Whatever peace or joy I may have for a while, I know I belong there, in the valley of Gehenna, because Te Ariki walks there till the world ends. God has gone deeper even than our despair. He chooses to live in Gehenna, in the acrid company of the true selves we cannot hide from him, though we hide them from other men and even disastrously from our own knowledge. His mercy raises the dead.

Here in this house I have the pain and peace of Lazarus. But the agony of Dives is what I felt in my dream: the plague city he calls a civilisation, a culture that cannot understand itself because it dare not accept its own spiritual strangulation and need of mercy. Instead it chooses guns and money and the badges of education. The agony of Dives is shaking the world to pieces. It is my leprous brother Dives whom I have to embrace, and that is why I shudder and cry out in my dreams.

God makes each thing and all things out of nothing. Nobody else can. We make something out of something—houses out of timber, or bread out of wheat. But the devil wants to imitate God. He makes a nothing out of nothing: that is, a lie. He has nothing positive to contribute, only wars, quarrels, lies, ulcers, deformations, the absence of good. Man is silly enough to imitate the devil. He too tells lies. A lie that is believed becomes an idol. Lies have an apparent positive reality. They provoke acts of fear and violence. Sincerity is no help. Most people sincerely believe the lies they tell and hear. We need truth. Sincerity comes from man; but truth comes from God.

Fear and anger are always absurd. They come from a misunderstanding of the nature of reality. Let us love the true self in each man: that is, the unborn Christ. Let us empty our hearts of possessiveness and receive through our senses what is, the pure and abundant creation that God made for us and for itself. Let us forget even the finest lies and accept the Word who is Truth springing up endlessly from the centre of our souls. Then we can be ourselves and live at peace with all men. The road is poverty.

Te Whiori
O Te Kuri

1

Two trucks pass me in a cloud of dust
As I come up the road from the river,

So I put the bathing towel over my mouth
And breathe damp cloth. Taraiwa on the old bridge

Is cutting the iron struts with a blow torch,
But he tells me—'Kua mutu'—'The oxygen is finished.'

I climb the long track to the wharepuni,
Meditating on the words of Thomas Merton—

'At the end of life God presses down a seal
On the wax of the soul. If the wax is warm

'It receives the mark; if not, it is crushed to powder'—
So be it. My own heart may yet be my coffin.

Up here they give me a cup of crushed apple pulp
To drink. In autumn the kai falls from the trees.

2

The dark light shines from the graves of the saints,
By which I mean the humble ones

Buried beside our house and under the bramble
That hides the fallen pas where sheep are grazing

And leave their clots of wool. The dark light shines
At the heart of the tangi where a tent has been put up

To hold the coffin, and a widow with a
Three-day-sleepless face is waiting for the

Resurrection. I remember
When the church was shut at Ngaruawahia,

Kneeling instead in front of the stone statue
Of Te Whaea, darkened by rain, eroded by moss,

Under an apple tree. The dark light shines
Wherever the humble have opened a door for it.

3

A giant weta climbs the curling ladder
Of the scrim beside my bed. I don't want

The scratching of this amateur bush demon
Interfering with my dreams,

Or love-bites on my neck. First Steve comes through
With a saw—'To cut him in half,' he says—

Then Zema—'You're piss-poor, Hemi,
At killing' (she giggles)—but I get a shoe

From the other room, stand on the strongest chair,
Wield it by the toe and belt him—crack!

The weta, trailing white guts, drops to the floor,
A three-inch dragon in his broken armour,

Poor creature! I finish him off with another blow
And lie back to read while the mosquitoes play their flutes.

4

The rain falls all day. Now the tanks will be full.
The road down river will turn to wet porridge

And the slips begin. Herewini told me
How Te Atua warned him that the bank would fall,

So he left the grader and came to shift his mates,—
They ran to safety and the bank did fall

Silently, eighty tons of earth and boulders,
Burying him to the armpits. His leg is still blue

Where the great stone cracked it and the bolts were put
    through the bone,
But he can walk on it. The drips from the holes in
    the roof

Spatter in the kitchen, on the boards behind the stove,
At the foot of Francie's bed. Beyond the lid of cloud

I hear the droning of the birds of Armageddon
That one day will end the world we understand.

5

The tribe in their own time are making a fowl run
Below the big chestnut. Therefore I wake

To hear the screech of nails being dragged with hammers
At the front of the house—Steve and Gregg

Doing what once would hardly happen
In two years. One by one the girls

Come in to visit their old hairy koro
On the broad of his back in a sleeping bag

Resting his rheumatism—Te Huinga,
Zema, Francie, Cam, they bring in coffee,

But stay to sit and open out their thoughts
And put their heads on my pillow. Some people think

I keep a harem. No; my back's not strong enough.
I keep a chook pen for birds of paradise.

6

'Te whiori o te kuri'—this is the tail of the dog
That wags at the end of my book;

After a dispute with one dear Maori friend
I walk all night on the road to Raetihi,

Thinking, 'Twenty-four miles will pulp the pads of my feet
Till the soles of them swell up like balloons;

'Pain in my feet; pain of my hara.' This morning
I saw the sun rise molten and red

Over the hill at Herewini's house
At Raetihi. But staggering on the stones

Last night, I had to stop, and looked up at the stars
And saw those ribs of white fire

Hung there like the underside of punga leaves
Planted for our human shelter.

7

To go forward like a man in the dark
Is the meaning of this dark vocation;

So simple, tree, star, the bare cup of the hills,
The lifelong grave of waiting

As indeed it has to be. To ask for Jacob's ladder
Would be to mistake oneself and the dark Master,

Yet at times the road comes down to a place
Where water runs and horses gallop

Behind a hedge. There it is possible to sit,
Light a cigarette, and rub

Your bruised heels on the cold grass. Always because
A man's body is a meeting house,

Ribs, arms, for the tribe to gather under,
And the heart must be their spring of water.

Glossary

ara	rise up
aroha	love
atua	spirit
Te Atua	God
e	O, oh
hangi	feast
hara	crime, fault
he	a, some
hinaki	eel-trap
hine	young woman
Hiruharama	Jerusalem
inanga	whitebait, also a pale translucent variety of greenstone
kai	food
kaore	no
karaka	a tree that bears edible berries
nga karakia	prayers
kare	ripple
Te Kare	a woman's name
kehua	ghost
ki	to, towards
kina	sea-egg
ko	introductory word indicating present tense
koe	you
kono	woven food basket
koro	uncle, elder relative
kua	introductory word indicating past tense
kuri	dog

mahi	work
Maoritanga	Maori spirit and tradition
mate	death, sickness
Maui	mythological Maori hero, one of whose exploits was to try to kill the Death Goddess by entering her body
mo	for
nga mokai	the fatherless
moko	facial tattoo
mutu	finished, completed—'Kua mutu' in Maori being the last words of Christ on the Cross
nga	the (plural)
ngakau	thoughts, heart
o	of
pa	Maori village
pai	good
pakeha	New Zealander of European descent
pataka	house for the storage of food
pia	beer
porangi	mad, madman
nga pukapuka	books
punga	treefern
Te Ra	the sun
Rahm	phonetic spelling of Ram, the Hindu name for God
rata	a New Zealand vine or tree with a brilliant red flower
Reneti	Lent
rite ki	like
riwai	potato

te taipo	the devil
taku	my
Tangaroa	Maori god of the sea
nga tangata	men
tangi	Maori funeral ceremony
taniko	Maori patterns of weaving with coloured thread, especially for cloaks and headbands
te	the (singular)
tenei	this
tino	very
toetoe	a New Zealand bush with a hollow stalk and whitish-yellow plumes
tuatara	a New Zealand lizard, famous for having a vestigial third eye in the back of its head
tuna	eel
tutua	slave, nobody
Wahi Ngaro	the Void, Space, a term used in Maori creation chants
wai	water
nga wai	waves
waiata	song
wairua	spirit, soul
weta	a New Zealand bush insect resembling a large grasshopper
Te Whaea	the Source, the Mother of God
whare	house
wharepuni	meeting house
whiori	tail
Te Whiro	Death